A
BETTER
YOU

A GUIDE INSPIRED
BY THE POWER
GREATER THAN
ALL OF US

Trishona Lindsay

Acknowledgements

I acknowledge with joy and pleasure:

God, for the wide availability of wisdom and instructions throughout my life, for the future and during this venture.

My parents for continuing to be the source of inspiration for me, for their support, love and motivation.

My special cheerleader/motivator and dear friends for surrounding me with unconditional love, laughter and just plain fun!

All those whose hearts are opening more and more each day from my encounter.

Foreword

Our Emotion is to be in line with God and what we are destined here on earth to become. Romans 12: 2 states, *"Be not conformed to this world, but be transformed by the renewal of your mind, that by testing you may discern what is the will of God, what is good and acceptable and perfect."*

We are here for a purpose, and without being emotionally intelligent we will not be able to accomplish our God given task.

Trishona Lindsay from a young age of seven years old had a love for God. Being in the Christian faith at twelve years of age, the journey was not easy, there were teething moments, as her mind was not yet conformed fully to God. In this book, Trishona Lindsay indicate some very important truth that will help each reader reflect on God's purpose for their life. She shares some of her experiences that can affect the average person and solutions that works.

I therefore recommend this book for those who dare to build their emotional intelligence and those who are struggling with their emotions so they can walk in the path that God through Jesus Christ have predestined.

- Prinella Scott-Lindsay (Teacher)
Jamaica Child Evangelism Fellowship

Giving her all, and expecting nothing in return, while touching other's lives in dramatic but profound ways has been the story of this author.

Hailing from that little rock called Jamaica, in the middle of the Caribbean Sea, a third world country with abject poverty in some quarters, and a high crime rate, wasn't enough to slow her pace, or to limit her scope, or to blot out her dreams for bigger things, and most importantly to encourage, enlighten and assist others to directing their paths to inner peace and a fulfilling life.

Having relocated to Canada, and now having opportunities and the world at her fingertips, Trishona Lindsay, a believer in Christ, but also a master in the management field, as well as a master logistics expert have not settled for success in her occupation but is still determined to achieve her goal of inspiring others.

It is with that life goal, and mission that she invites you to join her in taking this first step by reading this book, that promises to inspire and enlighten you, and assist in facing the challenges this life will throw at you.

It promises to be one that will show you other ways of coping with those pesky problems, and situations that we sometimes find ourselves in. I invite you to open your hearts and minds to receive what she has to offer, as we transcend to another dimension in this rather unrelenting world.

-Romaine Robinson
Motivator

Trishona had made the decision to give her life to the Lord Jesus Christ whilst in High School and this decision was a very serious one, as she was passionate about serving God. She was well supported by her parents, who had not given their lives to Jesus Christ in her early walk with God.

Trishona's love for Christ grew stronger and her desire was to fulfill the will of God for her life. I can remember when Trishona was immigrating to Canada, all she was saying was, "*I know this was the will of God for me to go*", despite how good she was doing in Jamaica she was very determine to follow the leading of God for her life.

In her book "A BETTER YOU", Trishona Lindsay wrote about how she held fast to the promises of God through the ups and downs and different kinds of difficult situations that tried to pull her away from the will of God for her life.

In this book, she shares her experiences and how to understand the control and power each person has within, to deal with all kinds of difficult situations that may arise and how to achieve self-actualization. Ultimately, A BETTER YOU.

I pray that this book will change you to be A BETTER YOU.

God bless you!

-*Patrick Lindsay* (Deacon)
Jubilee Christian International, Jamaica

Contents

Introduction

Many people believe that **IQ** intelligence is what determines success. However, researchers have consistently found that people with average **IQ's** outperform those with higher **IQ** 70% of the time.

Society does not seem to account for the main predictor as to why there is a disparity between a person who succeed and another who does not. We occasionally observe and can say supposedly that brilliant and well-educated people struggle, while others with fewer obvious skills or attributes flourish.

So, why is that? It turns out that the missing link in determining long-term success is **emotional intelligence** – a tried life compass, and frankly not everyone understands this!

Society tends to create a platform where people have the wrong perceptions about who they are and how life ought to be lived. This is not to condemn anyone, but to illustrate that many are doing the best they can. If each person knew better, they would have been more understanding and aware in order to create discovery for empowerment. Emotional intelligence links strongly with love and spirituality, bringing compassion and humanity in any relationship and/or situation. When Spiritual and Emotional Intelligence emerges, they assist in finding the deepest and most inner resource of an individual and their potential.

Studies have shown that people with high emotional intelligence:

• Experience higher levels of performance (for example high EQ customer service representatives outperformed others by approximately 30%)

• Experience higher levels of productivity.

• Experience higher problem-solving skills and lower levels of conflict.

• Are more effective leaders.

The problem is that for most of us, there was no one teaching or providing insight to us about our emotions and how they work. No one taught us that we can have more control over our emotions by developing awareness of our thoughts and feelings.

With that being said, this is the reason there are so many individuals experiencing:

• Being overwhelmed by life stressful encounters

- Getting carried away by negative emotional responses
- Feeling stuck when facing challenges
- Feeling socially awkward or having troubled relationships

As you work through this book, be reminded of the good news that emotional intelligence can be **DEVELOPED**!

It is not an inborn trait.

This book gives you a blueprint for improving and developing emotional intelligence, both INTRA-personal intelligences, or understanding of your own emotions, and INTER-personal intelligences, or understanding of others' emotions.

This book seeks to help you learn how to:

• Better understand the cause of your own emotions so you can shift your own emotional state.

• Eliminate negative emotions from early stages and avoid triggers, in order to prevent escalation.

• Reduce and release stress to better cope with life events.

• Develop healthy empathy so that you can better understand others without being sucked into their emotions.

• Listen and communicate effectively and tune into non-verbal communication and body language.

Developing and learning the skill of emotional intelligence is perhaps the most valuable skill anyone can EVER acquire.

Give yourself and your clients this gift!
Choose YOU!

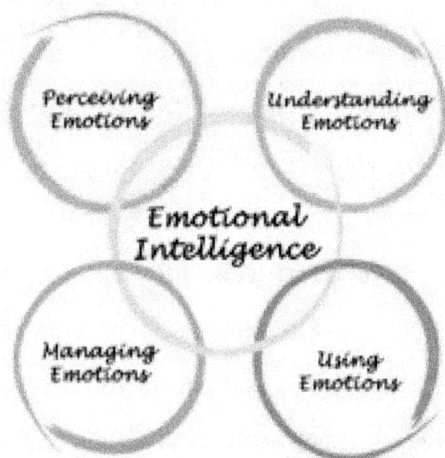

Chapter One

Identify
Unlimited Intelligence

"An intelligent heart acquires knowledge"

Life is inevitably unpredictable.

Emotions are never to be a guidance system. Instead we need to have wisdom to understand the thoughts and feelings to respond in certain situation.

As Proverbs 4:7 states, "Wisdom is the principal thing, therefore get wisdom: and with all thy getting get understanding."

We are responsible for the experience we attract. Some situations will unavoidably deter us from our ultimate desire and our peace, even though we have made a positive effort to be focused. For every habit and experience that repeats itself in and around your life, indicate there is a need within you for it. That need corresponds to some form of belief you may have.

When you can think upon the range of emotions that are expressed by individuals, you can confirm that no wonder they can get the better of us in every situation. This is because emotions without intelligence are referred to as "the works of the flesh".

We can agree there are so many synonyms to describe the feelings that surface in each person's life, yet they fall somehow in one of the following: fear, shame, worry, happiness, anger and sadness. At times, it can be so easy to forget that we have emotional reactions to almost everything that happens in our lives, whether we can easily notice them or not. The complexity of these emotions are revealed in their varying forms of intensity. We tend to focus on the situation and its impact on our life so much that we fail to pause in the midst and understand the underlying factor.

The works and/or performances of low or inexistent emotional intelligence are manifested through these:

1. Adultery – Adultery is a feeling that is performed by individuals with low intelligence emotionally. The scripture states in Proverbs

6:32, "But whoever commits adultery with a woman lacks common sense and sound judgement and an understanding, he who would destroy his soul does it." The lack thereof is as a result of the lack of moral principles and being emotional unintelligent.

2. Fornication – The feeling of being incomplete and the urge for faithless actions would lead a person to unintelligently emotionally act without instruction and wisdom. Not considering the negative impact or effect on their character or esteem.

These are some of the feelings that are exerted or performed from low and/or lack of emotional intelligence. If one would consider why there is a need for such misfortune, they would understand the insignificance of that feeling if they thought about it intelligently. These are emotional conditions that are not modified or adjusted by an intelligent factor and here we can see the need for emotional intelligence.

We battle with the challenging '*self*'", which can impact our success because the past, present and future tackles on what is important to us.

"*It is okay not to be okay*", the question is where you go from there?

When we realize that our brains are wired to make us emotional creatures, we get to understand that your first reaction to an event will always be an emotional one. Some experiences produce an emotion that you can easily concur; but at other times, these or this emotion may seem unrelenting. Let us take for instance fear and anxiety. We tend to correlate both emotions as they do ultimately occur together but they are not interchangeable. Fear would be considered having a known, or expected threat, whilst anxiety speaks to unknown, or unease relating to emotions and a stressor. In order for anyone to overcome this type of emotion, you first need to make that connection with God to receive true peace.

There are 5 steps to overcoming fear and anxiety (you can learn more by visiting www.coachedbytrish.ca). However, the hardest step is to identify the underlying factor that give rise to the fear and/or anxiety. When you have gathered a full understanding to the 5 steps, you will notice that the "heavy" and uncertain feeling has been lifted from your person and there has now been a new perspective to approaching the situation or project.

There are 4 parts of self that ultimately aligns our success. What are they you may ask?

Each of us has 1 or more of the 4 parts to our inner being. These parts include:

1. The part that seeks after the possibilities and changes.
2. The part that hastens into the new possibilities and changes.
3. The part that refuses to accept the need for the new possibilities and changes.
4. The part willing to adapt to the new possibilities with hope for greater success.

From the four parts, one needs to identify the dominant force that operates your inner being which will allow you to be in the know. The knowledge of what this force is, can offer invaluable ideas. Ideas to encourage, lift, control, and ultimately persevere.

"*Do not refuse
to change when
things change*"

We tend to recreate relationships based on the emotional environment of our early life. We focus on treating and expecting a certain acceptance of life in these relationships as what we once experienced from parents, family, and/or friends. What happened then cannot be used in today's situations.

Relationships are invaluable and open-ended. They should be treated delicately and should be lasting. Once you can identify the value of these relationships you become mindful of the impact that will or will not occur emotionally. In any case, be emotionally intelligent. Take the time to find yourself before you can give fully in any relationship.

"Be emotionally intelligent and operate in the inevitable."

Do not misunderstand the reactions but operate in the inevitable through intelligence. Think about the time you may or may not have had a boss or a partner who was like your mother or father?

Emotions always serve a purpose.

We are not victims; we are successors that believe in the power far greater than we are. We should flow through each moment and trust the power and intelligence to operate in the inevitable. We tend to have been berating ourselves for several years, asking, *'why me'*? But the real question should be *'why not me'?'*

Emotional Intelligence is a miracle cure. I am not referring to arrogance or egotistical attributes, that is only fear. I am referring to the respect and acceptance within our bodies and inner being.

Exercise: *I am*

A. Identify what is (are) the **dominant force** of your inner being which we identified earlier, taking into consideration all the relationships you are in (whether at work, home, personal, church, etc.).

B. Then **write down 33 ways** you can finish this sentence (*more space at the end of the chapter*)

"I AM.."

_____

_____

_____

_____

_____

The source of life itself

The power lift to greater success

The beauty within

The acceptance

Knowledge

The process of elimination

The way it works in completion.

-Trishona Lindsay

Continue "I AM…"

_____

_____

_____

_____

_____

_____

_____

_____

_____

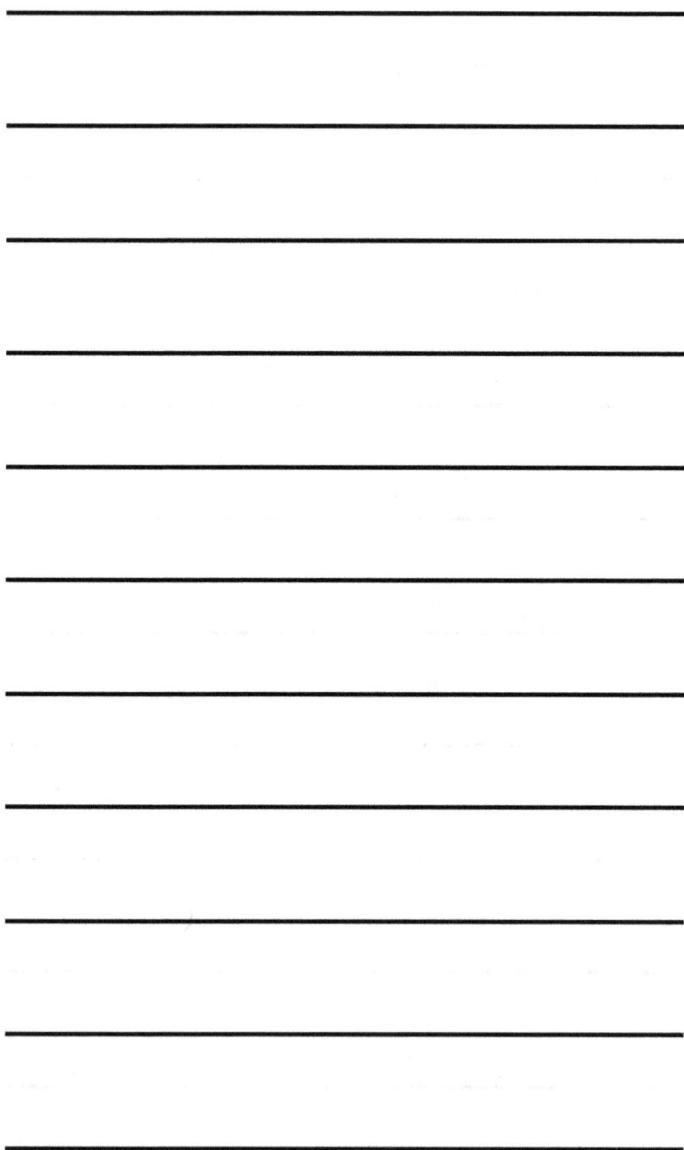

Chapter Two

Resistance
Change

"Change is never painful, only resistance to change bring forth pain"

The first step to healing or change is awareness.

In the chapter on Unmasked: 5 pillars to take your life on auto pilot, we illustrate in further details how to master and control each one.

Feelings are healing.

Healing is a condition.

Feelings must become subject to wisdom.

Healing from a situation can only be possible when we become aware of some buried patterns within us, whether emotionally or physically. We have the power to change our attitude towards any situation and/

or person in the past. However, we cannot change the past, it is over and done.

We tend to attract individuals in our lives that awaken the new way of approaching a dissolving problem. Often our first approach is to think this is silly or makes no sense and is unacceptable to our thinking. Our first resistance comes in play very strongly. This kind of response can be good as it can be the first step to healing.

We choose to believe that we are helpless victims and the power you give to the folly will be supported by the universe, as that is all they are drained with hearing. It is vital to release those foolish and negative intentions, as we also portray an image that the concept of what God has planned for us is against us. In all things, we need to know how to focus our minds on the healing work and dissolve that fear.

Write down three (3) conditions or situations you have experienced which you complained or have complained about.

_____

_____

_____

_____

Make the ultimate decision to change.

As humans, we often times prefer to have the situation linger. For transformation and intelligence to be the base of one's growth and achievement, we have to be willing to change, only then can inner and outer changes occur.

When you observe a rhythm or flow that derailed your ultimate decision, there is/was a pattern deeply buried that need or needed to be changed. The truth is that the process of changing only begins the very moment we acknowledge the need and the thought of making the change. Being impatient and creating constant excuses, are only forms of resistance. We need to understand that any reaction which you may feel, is illustrating that you are already in the process of healing, even if the total healing has not yet been completed.

Be in the rhythm to an everchanging life.
We fail to realize now is the time to acknowledge our responsibility for having created the situation or condition. However, I am not talking about that guilt feeling or about being regarded as a bad person. I am referring to the neglect or misconceptions that was exerted to have placed you in the process of healing.

I state this, to acknowledge the power within you that can transform your every thought into an experience. When you have acknowledged your responsibilities and learn how to use the power of emotional intelligence in positive ways for your benefit you will become more self-aware.

You all have lessons to learn, and the things which have become so difficult for you are only the lessons chosen for yourselves. When things are easy, there are no lessons being learned.

Have you ever thought about the hardest thing you have to get done and how much resistance **YOU** put up against it? Then you are looking at your greatest lesson!

Take the time to refrain resistance, and allow yourself to learn what it is you should learn from the situation, this will take you one step closer to self-awareness and making a change. Too often, instead of working on our changes, we decide to look at someone else's that need to changed. This too is a form of resistance. Resistance equal self-sabotage.

If you can't think on your common forms of actions and understand the fact that the simplest action can be categorized as a form of resistance, then let me illustrate. Resistance can be categorized in a number of ways, these include but not limited to:

• *Nonverbal actions*

These are daily impeding reactions to a situation and/or person despite the matter at hand. These include but not limited to: the constant procrastination and/or feeling/being sick.

- *Beliefs*

We develop certain perceptions to ideas based on how we were grown. Some of these perceptions become resistance to a change. These can be related to: how far you should live from work and about spiritual individuals should not be /get angry.

Interesting isn't it?

- *Assumptions*

There are situations where we may feel we must justify our actions and not realize we are typically resisting the change. This could be when you make certain statements daily or occasionally such as: only women drivers drive irresponsibly, they can't handle my anger and I don't want to disturb them.

- *Self-Concepts*

Having the ideas about ourselves that would cripple our success are used as forms of resistance and limitations, such as: saying I am too fat, I am too short and/or I am getting too old.

- *Denial*

  Creating the impression as though the need to change is not required as you have made all the necessary adjustments needed, is a form of resistance. Making excuses and saying things like: I can't do anything about the problem, I'll think about it tomorrow and/or as soon as I get back off the road I will do it.

These are examples of resistance and the list goes on and on.

Did you recognize any of these forms of resistance that you may have said or done? *For an exhaustive list (see section: forms of resistance).*

You may be wondering how does this relate to emotional intelligence. Well, being aware of who you are and the resistance you perform, knowing and unknowingly, places you one step ahead to developing your interpersonal skills for emotional intelligence.

During an encounter at work, there was a new immediate Director. In my opinion, his approach to management was domineering. I felt I was a target and I kept self-loathing on the fact that I had an ultimate goal and this person seem to be impacting it in some negative way. I would have a defensive approach to him at any chance I get. Was I emotionally intelligent or was I intelligent emotionally in my responses and ultimately my actions?

- Did I lead as how I should for my subordinates?
- Did I spend time to understand why I presume he was "domineering"?
- Was I wondering about the potential adjustments that I would need to implement?
- Was I being patient to the changes?
- Did I provide the same feedback as I would have before he was hired?

Out rightly no! Why? This is because in these cases, I was allowing the environmental factors to control my reactions and energy. So, I decided to further conduct a research, where I found the critical points and noticed the control I possessed. There I learnt I have the power within and started managing my micromanager.

It can be hard to make the changes we want to or should, but we try to make someone else change when he or she doesn't want to or don't see the need to and it can ruin a relationship, a friendship and an opportunity. Try to cross the bridge with joy and ease. Sometimes it is better to release the pattern and situation that has gotten worse over time. It's is not a bad thing but a sign that the situation is beginning to move. Your affirmations are working and you need to adapt and keep going.

"Try to cross the bridge with joy and ease"

Don't despair, but take it as a sign that the process you are experiencing is working. You begin to ask yourself "are you willing to give up toxic relationships? Are you willing to cut down on carbohydrates? Are you willing to venture in your own business and quit corporate? Why are you creating these relationships?"

As you approach the situations with affirmations you begin to say "I am willing to release the need for an uncomfortable relationship." This way you find that the toxic relationship no longer attracts you and the people in your life no longer share their criticism. Then you know you can reflect on the process of change and realize your inner guidance has led you to the stage of emotional intelligence.

There are stages for ultimate success to manage the upcoming changes. These become:

- Communication of the need for Change.
- Creating that coalition in any relationship and/or situation.
- Develop SMART goals and vision.
- Be empowered to take broad based actions.

- Generate the recognition of small but visible wins.

- Establish the sense of urgency for the need actualization.

- Develop new approaches for tackling these achievements for recurrence.

Exercise: *Releasing Needs*

Go to the mirror and look into your eyes for 5 minutes, think on something you want to change in your life. Then say out loud three times (3) with meaning - "I realize now that I created the condition and I am willing to release that pattern responsible for this condition."

If you are with a partner, have them tell you whether he/she thought you meant it. This is where you are convincing your partner. Ask even yourself after, whether you felt like you meant it. You can know this when the "heaviness" has lifted and you are now committed to passing through the resistance.

Exercise: *Overcoming Resistance*

Write down (3) moments you have or may have self-sabotage in any area of your life.

_____

_____

_____

_____

_____

_____

_____

The encouragement desired

The drive for greatness

The thought of increase and improvement

The joy within

-Trishona Lindsay

Chapter Three

Control
Power of Thoughts

"Thinking can be easy but acting may be difficult. Control is the feelings"

Emotions have permanent control on your every being. However, flexibility offers the opportunity to adjust your thoughts, feelings and behaviours to the unfamiliar, unpredictable and/or change the situations. No matter what the problem or situation may be, the only thing that any one person is dealing with is a thought and this thought can be changed.

When this is understood, you control the thoughts that follow an emotion, and you have a great deal of deciding how you react to an emotion as long as you are aware of it. Sanctified is a word that include emotional intelligence. This is where a person has control over their actions, thoughts and feelings.

Ask yourself….

- Are you more focused on the outcomes?

- Are you willing to acknowledge the need for change?

Let's consider the following, which of the statements resonate with you?

"People don't understand why I behave how I do?"
"People are out to get me?"
"People are considerate of my situation and/or opinion."

All of the above are feelings. Why? Self-hatred or limitations are only thoughts that one has about themselves. In this instance, that thought on anything good or bad produces feelings. When this thought produces feeling, one will tend to buy into the feeling. The only one thing a person have control over is your current thought. In essence, without a thought there is no feeling. So, believe it or not we choose and control our thoughts. The less of the self-hatred or self-restrictions for accomplishment, the more successful our lives become in every area and on all levels.

Wisdom and knowledge are open gateways to change and healing. Knowing that in any area of your life, whether in a relationship or a situation, what you give out is what you receive. Relationships provide benefits in multiple ways.

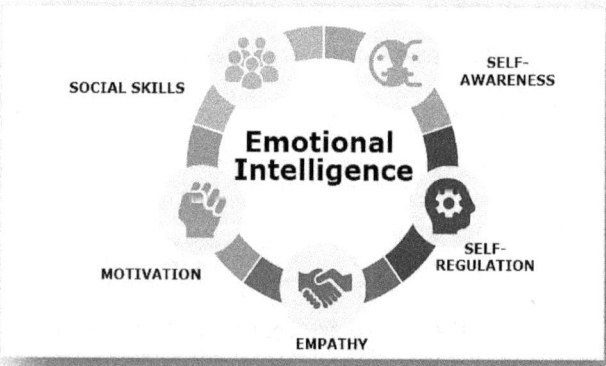

Finding that factor which magnetizes your energy, will provide you with the details about where you need emotional intelligence. This can influence how or what you think about yourself, and what you deserve in life or should become. This is just because stress builds on stress regardless of the source.

"Every thought

creates a future"

You must take accountability for what you have control over, and focus your energy on remaining flexible and open-minded in spite of the situation. Listen carefully and learn, that the only way to genuinely understand your emotions is to spend enough time thinking through them. This way you will figure out where they came from and why they are there.

What are you afraid/scared of? *additional space at the end of section*

What is/are your safety net? (*additional space at the end of section***)**

Your mind is a tool.

Incredible power and intelligence is within you. As you learn to control the thoughts and understand the choice of thoughts, you will be aligned with this power. Training the mind to chatter the old and maintain self-acceptance and approval are keys for positive changes. Despite the prevailing feeling of self-denial, mentally drape yourself to any immediate reaction contrary to change.

Fear can be a double standard.
Fear can be good, as it drives change and acceptance. However, it can drive pain, neglect, absorption and ultimately cripples the body physically, emotionally and psychologically.

You can incorrectly think that your mind runs the show but it is a tool for you to use as YOU wish. The thoughts that you choose to think create the experiences you encounter. When you have understood the power within, you will no longer be concerned about what you do or where you would have been if you weren't afraid.

Why not consider this as mental house cleaning? This is where you examine the past a bit more. Painful it can be, but why avoid addressing this issue now to avoid further despair? That underlying pain is the force to be "in control" of. Pick up the pain, polish it, refinish it or repair it.

Pain Factors

Take deep breaths and scan your thoughts.

Close your eyes and clear your mind. If you noticed any hesitation, **write down all** of the pain you are feeling or thinking on (*more space at the end of the chapter*).

Take your time. Be aware of the emotions you experience and take control over it.

_____

_____

Where it came from:

_____

_____

You may be concerned about the uncertainty of going through the change and learning emotional intelligence but taking control rather than settling is the key to success and manifestations.

Safety nets are the reflection of comfort zones. Test the situation or circumstance to know when it has become unbearable, toxic, or unrelatable. As the author, Spencer Johnson states in, "Who Moved My Cheese" - sniff the cheese often to know when it is getting old.

Overcome the fear and channel your energy in a new direction. Emotional intelligence is observed when you can laugh at your folly, the neglect, the misfortune, the pain (ultimately a setback/failure).

Identifying where you went wrong or what you did wrong. Translate the negative thoughts into neutral and positive statements and this will change the perspective of situations in your life or relationship.

In essence, emotional intelligence is the ability to recognize and understand the emotions in yourself and others, as well as the ability to use this awareness to manage your behavior and relationships in every situation. Avoid over-analyzing a failure. If there is a change, move past the inevitable. You will learn to keep things simple, flexible and adapt quickly.

Identifying and overcoming these pain factors (limitations) will transcend in the emotional intelligence to control your energy. We then recognize our magnificent power and importance to becoming divine.

Continue completing what you are *afraid/scared* of below:

_____

_____

_____

_____

_____

_____

_____

_____

Continue completing what are your *safety nets* below:

_____

_____

_____

_____

_____

_____

_____

_____

Continue completing the *pain factors* below:

_____

_____

_____

_____

_____

_____

_____

_____

_____

Continue completing *where the pain beliefs came from* below:

_____

_____

_____

_____

_____

_____

_____

_____

The things hoped for

The things accomplished

The battles overcome

The challenges accepted

-Trishona Lindsay

Chapter Four

Freedom
Envisioning Success

"*Everything is permissible for*
me"

Life can be simple, by fulfilling the promises ordained by God when you know and accept the possibilities of identifying your complacencies.

Every experience is considered a success.
But what does "*failure*" really mean?

Does it refer to the fact that something did not turn out the way you wanted? We out picture our inner thoughts and beliefs so perfectly, that we left the step out where you may have told yourself you did not deserve or you are not worth it.

Look ahead for change, even though you do not know what lies ahead. When you have refused to focus on the circumstances/relationship, you become aligned with your inner being and find a sense of control and calmness.

The only inhibitor to learning emotional intelligence lies within. Nothing is getting in the way of change until you have gotten better at releasing the unpleasant need. Continually adapt to learning to think in positive affirmations.

Yes, I know it is easier said than can be done, but I can assure you once you have started to create positive statements there is where the idea will stay. Too often, you would think in negative affirmations which only create more of what you say you do not want. Whatever you concentrate your interest or energy on is what increases. Avoid believing in limitations.

Demonstrating the results towards positive affirmations, you will see little miracles in your life.

I refuse to have any negative thoughts and I am in control of what I experience. Be grateful to the things you have is a step for developing emotional intelligence. When you practise blessing all areas in your life as well as expenses you have power over its impact. Bless the bills you pay and watch how you get rewarded unknowingly in other areas of your life. Be sure not to reject success.

"Knowing and accepting the possibilities identifies your complacency"

Upon learning to attract what I desire in my working environment I was in complete control. There I learned the reason I was overwhelmed and disturbed was as a result that I never understood the power within me and the importance of emotional intelligence to improving productivity. I was not excited, I was in complete "awe" of the process and how it manifested what I desired.

You can concur that life isn't fair, because there's nothing you can do about the misfortune, it really isn't up to you. When you were growing up, your parents would beat certain mantras in your heads.

However, what they forgot to explain after beating the mantras, was that you always have a choice. Believe it or not! You have a choice in how you respond to what may be before you in every area of your life and relationships. Even when you can't do or say anything that can change or influence the difficult situation, you always have a say in regards to your perspective of what is happening, what is going to happen and what will happen - which ultimately influences your feelings about it.

The principles of releasing the needs and learning emotional intelligence is mirrored as you plant "seeds" for success. These seeds will then grow abundantly.

When you find yourself in a position where you think you have no control, STOP and take a closer look at how you are reacting to the situation itself. Each time you feel an emotion starting to build up, STOP, take notice of it immediately. Ensure to refrain putting that "feeling" into the good or bad pile and take the time to remind yourself that this feeling is there to help you understand something important.

Find the time to suspend that judgement of the feeling or emotion and let it run its course to be in full control and freedom.

Consciously visualizing the abundance and success you desire, you are exercising the feeling for and of expansion and unlimited supply. Your prosperity consciousness is not dependent on money, but the flow of money within your life is dependent on your consciousness. Conceive more and more will locate you through faith and hope in God.

Recognize no matter how small the abundance may be, increase your consciousness by rejoicing in it. You should never want someone else's good. You want your good, even if you don't own anything. But that's only YET!

Emotional Intelligence fills your mind and overflows in the direction of progress.

There is a natural flow of life and understanding who you are through emotional intelligence you can develop intrapersonal skills to recognize, possessions are for a period of time and the power to birth your time is within you.

"Your prosperity is not dependent on money; the flow of money is dependent on your prosperity consciousness"

Exercise: *I approve of myself*

For at least a month (guaranteed), daily say for thirty-three (33) times the following, "*I love myself, therefore...*" finish the sentence in as many ways.

Ensure to write these down on a pad of paper for the next day until the end of the month. (*additional space at the end of the chapter*)

If you wish to work with a partner to hold each other accountable to making changes and learning emotional intelligence, you can hold hands and alternate say.

Exercise: *Envision the new*

Imagine having or doing something you are working towards for yourself. Ensure to fill in all the details relating to the desire, the feel, taste, touch and hearing. Take notice of others reaction to your practice of that change of state, ensure to make it okay no matter their reactions.

Continue completing "*I love myself therefore*"below:

_____

_____

_____

_____

_____

_____

_____

_____

The drive

The intentions

The win

The success

All determined from within

-Trishona Lindsay

UNMASKED

5 PILLARS OF
EMOTIONAL OPTIMAL FLOW

Pillar One
Self-Awareness

Self-awareness is the basis of emotional intelligence. When one can bring awareness and analysis to their own feelings and emotions, they are conscious and unconsciously taking control. Consciously, where you are aware of the pain, the hurt and limitations. Unconsciously, where you are under and not aware of the feelings or emotions.

Being aware of your mood and thoughts is where you successfully know, acknowledge and recognize your emotions. When you have recognized these feelings, you have developed the fundamental skills in emotional intelligence. Harnessing and perfecting this skill is paramount as every other emotional intelligence skill builds on the fundamental skill of self-awareness.

Once you have risen above the experiences, you are at a level of consciousness rather than being immersed in the emotions. If you can't notice your feelings, then you become a victim or at the mercy of the emotions.

We have crafter activities and mindful ideas to develop self-awareness successfully through Gods purpose and will for you (more details visit www.coachedbytrish.ca). These include:

- Daily reflection/Mindfulness Meditation
- Keep a vision board/ journal
- Get feedback
- Analysis tools such as Cognitive Behavioral Therapy

Pillar Two
Managing Emotions

Handling emotions is the key to self - regulation and/or self-management. Ensure that emotions do not concur or control your intelligence.

When you are able to handle the emotions, you ensure that you do not suppress the emotions selectively or make them inexistent.
It is like going to the shopping mall and without understanding how to manage emotions through emotional intelligence you unintelligently make a large purchase of items you necessarily do not need. The lack of logical thinking takes precedence in these cases.

To ensure these and more does not occur, you need to identify the key emotions that is appropriate to each relationship and/or situation. Defuse the challenging emotions that causes you to unintelligently operate in the present.

The activities we encourage to manage your emotions is through changing your physiology.

This is by practicing the powerful and simplest nuggets (more details visit www.coachedbytrish.ca).

These include:

- Power Nugget – high recognition of self
- Simple Nugget – daily mental adjustments

Pillar Three
Social Awareness/ Self-Motivation

The ability to apply intelligent emotions to life situation is when you harness the power of your emotions. If you don't control your emotions, it will control you. Out of control emotions has adverse harm on you and your relationships or in any situation. When you have harnessed this power, you are able to use your emotions to achieve the goals and birth your vision/affirmation you desire as well as motivate yourself to achieve the most out of your mental capabilities.

Being able to function and increase level of productivity in the face of adversity and obstacles is the key to high performance. Ensure to exercise enthusiasm and persistence.

We only limit ourselves from achieving because of our emotions. Our emotions will diminish your performance.

Through social awareness and self-motivation, this is where you achieve greatest accomplishment from practicing impulse control and delayed gratification.

We tend to perform so much better when under stress/anxiety of forceful achievement or increase interest for change.

The activities and testing we recommend to handle emotions include:

- Marshmallow test
- Reframing
- Deep Breathing Exercise
- Practicing Optimism
- Operating on Optimal Flow

With these testing you will be able to achieve the goal of self-imposed delay of any form of gratification (more details visit www.coachedbytrish.ca).

Pillar Four
Relationship Management

A person battling with insecurity can be a challenge. However, to successfully manage the relationship, you need emotional intelligence. You would need to be the most powerful person in the relationship and deescalate their emotions rather than escalate.

But how is this done? This is mastering pillar number one. Once you have become aware of your emotions and can identify others emotions you have become emotionally intelligent in tuning into others emotions.

There are certain abilities necessary for successfully garnering interpersonal intelligence in any relationship. First you need to learn how to negotiate, how to develop personal connection, how to coordinate the efforts of people and how to analyze and dissect situation at hand by social analysis.

Don't be misguided by the fact that while understanding all these, ensure it is in alignment with the purpose and will of God as well as your feelings not matter the situation at hand.

Pillar *Five*
Empathy

The ability to intelligently recognize and respond to the emotions of others is referred to as empathy. A great example is in the bible where Jesus was being mocked by everyone. However, his reaction was priceless. This is because he did nothing. This is the epiphany of emotional intelligence. The most important thing is that empathy actually build on self -awareness. Jesus was able to earn the respect by responding to his feelings and exert empathic reactions to their actions. He was able to understand not only his emotions but their emotions and react accordingly. The more one is able to understand their emotions, you are able to read and feel them in others. You build rapport, become sensitive and outgoing.

To exercise and master empathy amongst group and/or peer, you can perform the empath exercise. This exercise is where you analyze the emotions of others non-verbal actions.

For more implementation plan of this exercise you may visit www.coachedbytrish.ca.

FORMS OF RESISTANCE

1. <u>Passive Resistance Change</u>

This form of change refers to individuals who are aware of the need to change or silent to the need to change but never act on them. This illustrate the fear manifesto, and the person who enters a stage of fight, fright and flight. This person would need to understand why a change is required and how to get away from the delay or having the fear negatively impact them. There are instances where aspects of Overload Resistance are prominent. This is where the proposed change may make you feel heavy or uncomfortable and at times, it may be to your sense of competence or confidence, or possibly your imagination of a future situation in a way that may or may not turn out well for you.

Having an understanding that fear does not only arise in the face of a real threat, it also arises in the face of the imagined threats or unease is paramount for overcoming the passive resistance to change.

2. Active Resistance Change

This form of resistance refers to individuals that act against a change, overtly or covertly with the intent to focus on negatively influencing others to also be in a state of resistance. This individual may have challenge themselves or others depending on their level of confidence. The cause of any individual exerting active resistance is usually as a result of a threat response where they are prompt in modelling a sense of "fight" in all cases. This is where you may feel out of control and unfairly treated in any situation and the "fight" response is in an attempt to reassert that loss autonomy.

This action is as a result that it may be in conflict with something that has a dominant hold over one's beliefs or priorities (e.g. you are trying to change something you think your boss is against). Generally, you will notice this obvious active change resistant behaviour when the impact of the change in any area of your life is imminent. Let's say for instance e.g. when you are trying to force a commitment, or when you are suggesting things up the line into the view of your superiors at work.

3. Attachment Resistance Change

This form of resistance refers to individuals that oppose strongly against change with the attempt to convince others to be radical in their efforts. They try to minimise the situation, problem or circumstance in order to maintain a status quo. However, if they noticed that the change is inevitable or required, they will suggest or propose a slight change or adjustment to achieving the need/change while still maintaining their status quo.

This action is caused by have that strong sense of ownership for any form of underlying process or factors that they have strong emotional ties to. Whenever a person is heavily invested in an existing way of resolving that situation or problem their thinking is locked around that known process.

4. Uncertainty Resistance Change

This form of resistance refers to individuals that spends a lot of their time worrying, hypothesising on the need to change and its ultimate impact on any area of their life. They tend to decline in their level of productivity as they find difficulty rising above the negative influence that may surround them on a daily basis.

This action is caused when the level of uncertainly is heightened and one is constantly working to make sense of the problem, situation or circumstance around them. In most cases, there may be gaps in that they would need to fill and this can lead to wasted efforts on things that may not happen. With this added situation and the other circumstance, they may be driven to resisting the change and its need in any area of their lives.

5. Overload Resistance Change

This form of resistance refers to an individual who focuses on the unexpected emotional impact about the change. In essence, to the individual it may seem as pushing back at the need to change but having no particular argument about the change itself.

This action is quite common especially in workplaces where change is a regular process for many years in one form or another. The change may be considered as normal but the frequency of this change occurring in regular life is not as constant as experienced within organisations. With that being said, the pace at which it occurs, is quite high in comparison and the many are instigated with no influence on those whom are mostly affected.

WHEN & WHY
THIS BOOK
WAS WRITTEN –
Afterword

In November 2018, I spent two weeks fasting and verbalizing positive affirmations because I needed a change, I needed to have a sense of fulfillment. I needed to release a need that was crippling my self-actualization.

I wrote on a pad of paper and kept inside the house and a copy inside my vehicle to repeat daily. Here is a significant portion of what I wrote that day, *"Lord, I thank you for life and its many experiences. I thank you for favor ahead of situations. I am gifted and talented. I am beautiful and guided as I hold fast to your promises for my future. I can and will be a change and make an impact."*

It was profound to me at that moment and because I am a person that believe God will only bless me with the desires of my heart. I was able to daily tap

www.ingramcontent.com/pod-product-compliance
Lightning Source LLC
Chambersburg PA
CBHW061503040426
42450CB00008B/1469